WESSEX BUSES
1970–1985
MAINLAND NATIONAL
BUS COMPANY FLEETS

MALCOLM BATTEN

AMBERLEY

First published 2019

Amberley Publishing
The Hill, Stroud
Gloucestershire, GL5 4EP

www.amberley-books.com

Copyright © Malcolm Batten, 2019

The right of Malcolm Batten to be identified
as the Author of this work has been asserted in
accordance with the Copyrights, Designs and
Patents Act 1988.

ISBN 978 1 4456 9487 0 (print)
ISBN 978 1 4456 9488 7 (ebook)

British Library Cataloguing in Publication Data.
A catalogue record for this book is available from
the British Library.

Orgination by Amberley Publishing.
Printed in the UK.

Contents

Introduction

The bus scene around Southampton and its surrounding towns in the 1970s and early 1980s saw great change. The National Bus Company had been set up on 1 January 1969 as part of the 1968 Transport Act. This brought together the already nationalised Transport Holding Company fleets and the former British Electric Traction (BET) fleets. The main operator in south Hampshire was THC fleet Hants & Dorset. Its area stretched from Gosport in the east to Poole in the west. To its north was fellow ex-THC fleet Wilts & Dorset. Centred on Salisbury in Wiltshire and working westwards into Dorset from here, it also served Andover and Basingstoke in Hampshire. As THC fleets, they had largely standardised on vehicles with Bristol chassis and ECW bodywork – both nationalised companies which had been restricted to selling to the nationalised bus companies until 1968. Under National Bus Company control the green buses of Hants & Dorset were merged with the red buses of Wilts & Dorset under the Hants & Dorset name in October 1972. They had already been under common management since 1969 and the fleets were renumbered into a common sequence in September 1971.

Variety came in April 1973, when the much-loved independent operator King Alfred Motor Services of Winchester sold out to Hants & Dorset. Initially, many of the acquired buses continued to operate and were given NBC livery. But within a couple of years these non-standard vehicles were phased out as standard Leyland Nationals and Bristol VRs entered the fleet.

A small expansion to the west came in January 1974 when the Swanage operations of Western National were transferred to the company. However, on 25 July 1976 the combined bus and coach station in Bournemouth was gutted in a tragic fire that destroyed ten H&D vehicles plus eight Western National coaches parked there. The site was not rebuilt and this deprived us of an excellent location for photography.

The introduction of the NBC corporate livery from 1972 deprived us of the previous variety. Although the green buses of Hants & Dorset were in the majority, NBC poppy red was adopted rather than the alternative of leaf green.

Under the NBC, new vehicles in all its fleets became largely standardised with the Bristol VR as the main choice for double-deckers, and the Leyland National and Bristol LH becoming the predominant single-deck choice. However there were severe economic difficulties at the time, due to industrial relations troubles and the effects of the three-day week. New vehicles had long delivery times and spares became hard to get. Both the Hants & Dorset and Wilts & Dorset companies had an ageing fleet with no double-deck vehicles suitable for one-person operation at the outset of the 1970s. The NBC drafted in vehicles from other fleets around the country to modernise the fleets, many of these coming from ex-BET fleets and so being of unfamiliar manufacture. The main garage at Grosvenor Square, Southampton, behind the coach station, was also the dumping ground for withdrawn vehicles, and the open yard was always worth a photographic visit, which, as I was living in Southampton at the time, I would regularly do.

One solution was to order Bedford or Ford buses, which had a shorter delivery time span. In August 1973 H&D ordered twenty Ford R1014s with ECW bodywork – the first time ECW had bodied Fords. The order was increased to twenty-five and the vehicles started arriving a year later in August 1974.

In April 1983 it was all change for a second time when Hants & Dorset was split up again. This time it became Hampshire Bus and Wilts & Dorset. However, the boundaries were different to the former companies, better reflecting their trading names. Hampshire Bus took the Basingstoke area (in Hampshire) while Wilts & Dorset now took on Bournemouth, Poole and Swanage (in Dorset). Coaches were hived off to a separate company using the existing coach fleet name of Shamrock & Rambler. They were to be further divided in 1984 with Southampton-based coaches becoming Pilgrim Coaches.

Another independent company had been the Gosport & Fareham Omnibus Co. (trading as Provincial), who sold out to the NBC in January 1970. They had a very old and distinctive fleet, with such rarities as Guy Arabs with Deutz air-cooled engines and Reading bodywork. Modern vehicles included examples of the uncommon (and unreliable) Seddon Pennine IV chassis. The NBC decided heavy investment was needed here and after a raft of second-hand vehicles were drafted in to replace the worst of the old stock, the company then received the first batch of the new standard Leyland Nationals in Hampshire and a new bus station was built at Gosport in 1972. NBC leaf green was adopted for this fleet, which retained its separate identity although head office administration was transferred to Bournemouth along with that of H&D and W&D.

From 1983 Provincial came under common management with Hampshire Bus, but retained its separate identity and NBC green livery. It also gained the Fareham area routes and vehicles from Hants & Dorset.

Former BET fleet Southdown was the company fleet serving Portsmouth, and the Sussex coast right through to Eastbourne. They also got round the north of Portsmouth Harbour to reach as far west as Fareham. From 7 March 1976 the new 'Solenteer' service, X71, worked jointly with Hants & Dorset, connected Southampton with Portsmouth and Southsea.

In Dorset, as mentioned above, the Swanage area had been an outpost of Western National until this was transferred to Hants & Dorset. Rural mid-Dorset was served by the independent Bere Regis & District. Western National resumed at Weymouth, terminus of the main line from London Waterloo, until July 1967. It was the last steam-worked main line in the country. Its territory would stretch all the way to Cornwall (except for parts of Devon served by Devon General). Before the NBC it had traded as either Southern or Western National depending on whether the area in question was previously reached by the former Southern or Great Western Railways – these parts of Dorset would have been Southern National. Under NBC ownership all licences were placed under the Western National name, although vehicles could still be seen with Southern National fleetnames until they were repainted or the NBC style was applied. Western/Southern National also owned Royal Blue – the trading name for coach services from London and elsewhere to Hampshire and all points west to Cornwall. Under the National Bus Company all express coach services would eventually come under the National Express brand with a common white livery.

From 1 January 1983 it was all change for Western National too. Like Hants & Dorset, it was split up in anticipation of later privatisation. The Dorset and Somerset area became Southern National, reusing a name from the past, while Western National became the Cornwell area. Devon General returned to being a separate company (having been under common management) and a new company, North Devon (trading as Red Bus), served the northern part of Devon around Barnstable. From 1985 it would be all change again. The Conservative Government of Mrs Thatcher took a different approach to the provision of public transport from its predecessors. In would come deregulation, with open competition allowed on profitable services and route tendering on subsidised routes. The National Bus Company fleets would be privatised and local authority fleets put up for sale. But that is another story and beyond the scope of this book.

All photographs are by the author.

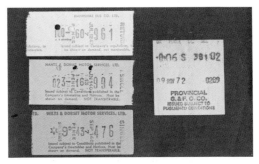

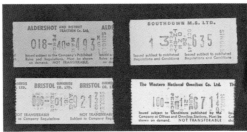

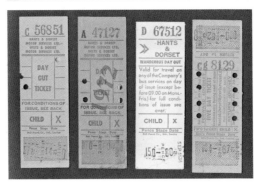

Hants & Dorset to Renumbering, September 1971

The Hants & Dorset fleet in 1970 still included large numbers of Bristol KS and KSW types dating from 1950–2, both full-height and lowbridge models. The highbridge models were the mainstay of the services linking Bournemouth and Poole. KSW6B No. 1307 is on a local service to Wallisdown Estate at Bournemouth bus station on 3 March 1971.

When the low-height Bristol Lodekka was introduced, this did away with the need for lowbridge buses with their sunken gangways and four-in-a-row seating upstairs. Bristol LD6G 1434 stands outside Southampton garage in February 1971.

Hants & Dorset had an arrangement with Bournemouth Corporation since 1919 whereby the corporation buses did not serve Poole and, in return, Hants & Dorset services running east from Bournemouth did not carry local passengers within the Bournemouth area. Bristol LD6G 1432, en route to Lymington, carries a slipboard on its radiator stating 'Not on service for Bournemouth Corporation passengers'. 5 May 1971.

The most modern double-deckers in 1970 were 1968-built Bristol FLF6L (Leyland 0600 engine) 1573–7. Nos 1574–5 were based at Winchester, where 1575 is seen laying over on trunk route 48 to Southampton. 17 March 1971.

Another FLF, although this time with the more common Gardner engine and therefore a FLF6G, was 1557, noted at Bournemouth in May 1971. Like 1575, it has the Cave-Brown-Cave heating and ventilation system and the grilles for this are either side of the blind box. This was developed at Southampton University and first trialled by Hants & Dorset in 1953. All Lodekkas delivered from the end of 1961 onwards had this feature.

1206 was a rare example of the Bristol FL (30 ft, rear entrance). This was the least common of the four versions produced of the F series Lodekkas and H&D had twelve of these. It was seen at Bournemouth in May 1971. Note the illuminated offside advert panel – a feature also found on some London Routemasters of the same period.

Withdrawn and awaiting disposal at Southampton, KEL 406 was a Bristol LL6B built in 1950. Originally it had a half-cab coach body built by Portsmouth Aviation, but in 1960–2 the batch was rebuilt with ECW full-front bus bodies. The upswept rear end was to provide clearance on the ramp of the Sandbanks Ferry, which they crossed on route 7 Bournemouth–Swanage. 28 October 1971.

As with other THC companies, Hants & Dorset downgraded some former Bristol LS and MW coaches for bus work. 878 was a 1961 MW6G. Although retaining coach seats, it was now fitted with route blinds and a 'pay as you enter' sign. It was seen at Eastleigh on 14 February 1971.

883 was another MW6G with the later style ECW coach body, now downgraded and painted in dual-purpose livery. It was at Bournemouth working on route 7 to Swanage – not the normal type of vehicle for this route. 31 May 1971.

During 1967–8, before the Bristol LH model came on stream, a number of THC companies bought some lightweight Bedford buses. Hants & Dorset was one of these, taking Bedford VAM chassis with either Strachans or Willowbrook bodies. Nos 3001–10 had forty-seat dual-door Willowbrook bodies with cutaway front ends for the Sandbanks Ferry, replacing the Bristol LLs seen earlier. 3009 loads at Bournemouth on 26 May 1970.

Bristol's rear-engined RELL model entered the fleet from 1968. No. 3019 of 1969 had an ECW B45D body with dual doors and was seen at Gosport in October 1970.

At Southampton coach station, which backed onto the garage, is one of H&D's Bristol MW coaches, No. 896. 12 May 1971.

Coaches also ran in the orange and cream livery of Shamrock & Rambler, a company taken over by the THC in 1966, and whose eight Southampton-based vehicles were transferred to H&D in 1969. No. 931 was a Bedford SB5 with Duple body dating from 1963. It was one of a pair originally with Harris, Cambridge, and was at the Southampton garage on 13 February 1971. Alongside is a Royal Blue Bristol MW.

Withdrawn and dumped at Southampton in February 1971 was No. 927 (605 LJ), a 1961 AEC Reliance with Duple Britannia C37F body.

Most bus companies retained an old bus or buses for driver training. At the Southampton garage was this Bristol K5G, No. 1116. The chassis dated from 1946, but its lowbridge fifty-three-seat body dated from 1940. It had been a training vehicle since 1964.

Wilts & Dorset to Renumbering, September 1971

As with H&D, most of Wilts & Dorset's buses were Bristols and there were no double-deck vehicles suitable for one-person operation. Bristol LD6G 604 is on a Salisbury city service. 13 February 1971.

Bristol FLF6B 686 was seen 'off territory' on rail replacement work at Reading General station on 27 March 1971.

Seen withdrawn at Salisbury garage in May 1971, 559, registered LAM 109, was one of fifteen Bristol LWL5G models bought in 1954. These were the last of the type to be made, when Bristol had already been building the replacement underfloor-engine LS model for two years. Originally they had half-cab rear-entrance bodies, but between 1958 and 1960 the company rebuilt them with front entrances and full fronts, as seen, for one-man operation.

533 was a bus-bodied Bristol LS6G, but like many in the fleet it had coach-style seating and so the body code was DP39F. It was at Salisbury bus station on 16 May 1971.

In 1963, Wilts & Dorset had acquired the fleet of Silver Star, Porton Down. The fleet was mainly Leylands and so most vehicles were not retained as being non-standard. However three Leyland Tiger Cub buses with Harrington bodywork were kept and would pass to Hants & Dorset in 1972, along with three Leyland coaches. 559 was originally Silver Star 33 and dated from 1958. The 'peak' on the dome was where the star emblem of Silver Star was originally displayed.

As with Hants & Dorset, W&D bought some Bedford VAM buses in 1967–8. Strachans B41D-bodied 813 backs into the H&D garage at Winchester on 24 August 1969. Dual doorways were something of a fad in the bus industry in the mid- to late 1960s, but can hardly be justified on vehicles like this used on mostly rural routes.

Arriving in Winchester from Salisbury on 17 March 1971 is Bristol RELL6G No. 844. Again, it is fitted with dual-door bodywork.

Another RELL6G, but this time with dual-purpose fifty-seat body and taken in Salisbury garage in May 1971.

Like its neighbours, W&D bought a number of Bedford coaches. HAM 505E was a Duple-bodied VAM14, seating forty-one. On 10 July 1971 it was at London's Victoria Coach Station, on hire to Royal Blue for a summer extra relief working.

Hants & Dorset/Wilts & Dorset From Renumbering 1971–2

In September 1971 a new common numbering system was adopted. Former W&D vehicles were numbered in blocks under 1000 according to type. The oldest vehicles in the fleet, Bristol K and LS types, were numbered with the newest vehicle taking the highest number in the block, e.g. 399 for the newest KSW and so backwards. Former H&D vehicles took similar blocks but in the range from 1000–1999. The old numbers had been applied on cast plates, painted in different colours to indicate the garage to which a vehicle was allocated. Thus, black letters on a yellow background was for Southampton, white on blue was Winchester, etc. Now the numbers would be cheaper stick-on numbers and the garages were shown by coloured spots. There were three areas: Eastern, Western and Northern. The main garage in each area had a single coloured spot – Southampton = yellow, Poole = white and Salisbury = blue respectively, while subsidiary garages carried the area colour and a second spot.

Sporting its new number – 1834 – and garage spots, this former Bristol MW6G coach at Bournemouth differs from 7119 LJ seen earlier in that it is now fitted with bus seats and is in the bus livery. 15 June 1972.

The first one-person-operated double-deckers to enter the fleet arrived in 1971 when six Daimler Fleetline CRG6LXB buses with Roe bodies were supplied. They had originally been ordered for the Provincial fleet but were diverted in exchange for six Bristol RELLs. Two of the Fleetlines were initially sent to Southampton where they worked routes 54 and 88, which were jointly worked with Southampton Corporation (who used Leyland Atlanteans). 1905 is at the Southampton Central station terminus on 12 January 1972. The others went to Poole to replace the last of the highbridge Bristol K types.

In order to modernise the aging fleet, the NBC transferred a batch of thirty-three Leyland Panther PSUR/1R buses with Willowbrook bodywork from Maidstone & District in 1972. Two of these, JKK 205/187E, are seen on arrival at Southampton garage on 27 January. The Panthers were divided between the H&D and W&D fleets.

The Panthers entered service in a variety of liveries. 1689 carried Hants & Dorset green when noted at Winchester on 8 June 1972. It was originally Maidstone & District 3084.

By contrast, 690 was one of sixteen for Wilts & District and painted in its Tilling red livery. It is arriving at Basingstoke on 24 March 1972.

1697 was one of four buses that entered service retaining their Maidstone & District livery. It was taken at Southampton's West Marlands bus station (since closed) on 3 July 1973. By now NBC-style fleetnames were being applied to the bus fleet.

Typifying the vehicles now being replaced are these 1953-built Bristol LS6Gs, MLJ 148/6, and KEL 715, a 1950 KS6B with lowbridge body. They were delicensed at the Grosvenor Square garage, Southampton, on 1 May 1972.

There were still many old vehicles in both fleets. Wilts & Dorset was running four of these 1950 Bristol LL6Bs, rebodied in 1961/2, that had been transferred from the H&D fleet in 1970. 723 was on school bus duties at Basingstoke on 24 March 1972, although they were also used on some stage services, including route 107 to Alton. The last of these veterans survived into 1973.

Many Bristol K types also remained, such as W&D 371, a 1952 KSW5G, also at Basingstoke the same day.

Another vehicle seen at Basingstoke on 24 March 1972 was 833, a dual-purpose Bristol MW6G dating from 1966.

Now carrying new number 1515, the last of the Willowbrook-bodied Bedfords disembarks from the Sandbanks Ferry on 22 January 1972, having allowed the cars off first.

Both fleets contained a number of Bedford VAL coaches with their distinctive twin-steer arrangement. H&D 1056 with Duple bodywork was at Victoria Coach Station on 15 April 1972.

Hants & Dorset 1972–83

In October 1972 the fleets of Hants & Dorset and Wilts & Dorset were merged under the Hants & Dorset name. NBC corporate livery of poppy red was adopted for buses while coaches generally adopted the National white livery. The coaches running under the Shamrock & Rambler name were transferred to National Travel South West in 1973.

The new look. Former W&D Bristol FS6G 106 displays NBC red and the blue spot for Salisbury garage at its home city in March 1973.

With the introduction of the NBC livery, for a while you could see vehicles together in all three liveries, as here with these Lodekkas at Basingstoke in April 1975. Note also that the middle Lodekka has a second cream band below the upper deck windows – a feature discontinued by H&D.

Former W&D vehicles were given Hants & Dorset NBC-style fleetnames on their sides, but often retained the Wilts & Dorset name on the front, as with MW6G 802 at Andover in March 1973.

Bristol LS 1783 (SRU 973) was transferred from the H&D fleet to Wilts & Dorset and repainted in Tilling red. After October 1972 it regained the Hants & Dorset name but in NBC style, while still carrying Wilts & Dorset on the front. Seen at Salisbury, 4 September 1973.

There are always exceptions, and Bedford VAL 60 was still displaying full W&D identity when photographed at Southampton garage in March 1973. Its sister alongside does seem to have gained an NBC fleetname though.

Displaying an NBC-style fleetname on a white livery with poppy red skirt and lining is 19 (HAM 504E), a former W&D Bedford VAM14 with Duple body. It was at the Winchester coach station in June 1973. At that time, this location could provide a fascinating mix of vehicles in a variety of liveries from all over the country on a daily basis.

1509 was a unique ex-H&D Bedford VAM in that it was the only single-door example, and its Willowbrook body had gained a new front end. It was caught departing Bournemouth bus station on 8 November 1972 when still in full original livery.

The Bristol VRT had been in production since 1969, but Hants & District did not receive any until late 1972 when a batch of six were sent to Basingstoke. 3305 leaves the combined garage and bus station on a local service in April 1973. These were the first buses to be delivered in the new NBC poppy red livery. New vehicles were numbered in the 3000–3999 range.

Also sent to Basingstoke were six Metro-Cammell-bodied Leyland Atlanteans, received from Maidstone & District in 1973. 3999 was seen there in April 1975. One was only used for spares – the others moved on to Western National in 1976.

These were not the only Leylands to enter the fleet in 1973! First to arrive were five 1966 Leyland Leopards with Duple bodies from North Western, FJA 225–9D. 3002 was in the yard at Southampton on 3 July.

The Leyland National was designed in conjunction with the NBC as a standard bus for its fleets. Hants & Dorset received its first examples, 3601–4, in 1973. 3603 loads for Hamble at Southampton on 18 May.

Other Bristols arrived, including one last batch of RELLs before the Leyland National superseded these, and nearly eighty further examples of the LH model between 1973 and 1975. One of the first batch from 1973, No. 3509 was seen in Salisbury bus station on 4 September.

Most bus fleets retained an old bus or buses as driver training vehicles, but a conductor training vehicle was something of a rarity. This former Bristol LS coach, now numbered 9095 and seen at Southampton in February 1973, had probably been introduced in connection with the changeover to decimal currency in 1971. Conductors would be needed until the last Lodekkas left the fleet in 1980.

On 29 April 1973 the Winchester-based independent operator R. Chisnell & Sons Ltd, trading as King Alfred, sold out to Hants & Dorset after experiencing staffing and maintenance difficulties. They operated all the local services as well as some country routes. Thirty buses and coaches plus seven Ford Transit minibuses were taken over, bringing more variety to the fleet. One of four Roe-bodied Leyland Atlanteans was seen at the back of the King Alfred garage, displaying its new number 2301 and H&D legal lettering, on 8 September. The Atlanteans were later transferred to Bournemouth and Poole.

Four AEC Bridgemasters came from King Alfred. Nos 2201–2 were given NBC fleetnames but were withdrawn without being repainted into poppy red, being the last vehicles to retain King Alfred livery. No. 2002 was seen in the Broadway, Winchester, in August 1974, from where King Alfred services departed. The former routes were renumbered in the 170s/180s.

Other vehicles, including the two AEC Renowns, were repainted, but some needed some major attention first. 2211 (595 LCG) is seen awaiting attention at Winchester garage on 7 March 1974.

Sister vehicle 2212 was in better condition and was repainted in 1973, as seen here on 2 September 1976.

Oldest of the vehicles to be repainted were the two dual-purpose Weymann-bodied Leyland Tiger Cubs dating from 1957. 2701 is seen in the bus station, which was not served by King Alfred vehicles during the company's independent days. They were withdrawn in 1975.

Three 1962 Willowbrook-bodied Leyland Leopards were acquired and 2651 shows off its new colours on 8 September 1973. Most of the ex-King Alfred buses would be withdrawn within two years, replaced by standard Leyland Nationals, Bristol VRs and LHs.

The three newest buses in the King Alfred fleet were a trio of Metro-Scanias dating from 1971. These were not retained by Hants & Dorset, instead being transferred to London & Country at Stevenage. Here they joined four similar vehicles which were bought for comparison trials with Leyland Nationals and AEC Swifts. They were painted, like the others, in Superbus livery and AOU 110J is at the bus station in September 1974.

To replace them, Hants & Dorset received three dual-door Leyland Nationals from London Country, Nos 3625–7, NPD 108/10/11L. These had not actually worked for London Country, having been on loan to Nottingham Corporation while that company's own Nationals were awaited. 3625 backs out of Winchester bus station on service 69 to Fareham via Bishops Waltham on 7 December 1974.

While the ex-King Alfred vehicles were being patched up and repainted, some older vehicles were drafted in to cover services. 1384 (KRU 987) was a 1952 Bristol KSW6B, seen blinded for former King Alfred route 18 on 1 October 1973.

Also drafted in was the last Bristol LS bought by Wilts & Dorset. 799 dated from 1956 and was working King Alfred route 8/9 to Stockbridge and Broughton on 1 August.

Two Bristol LD5G Lodekkas were sourced from Eastern National. 3499 (ex-ENOC 2429 of 1955) is seen in the garage yard with one of the former King Alfred Tiger Cubs on 2 August 1974. 3499 was notable as the only vehicle in Tilling green livery with a second cream band – a feature phased out by H&D in the 1960s.

Four coaches came from King Alfred and all were retained by their new owners. JHO 702E, a Plaxton-bodied Bedford VAM14, was located at Southampton on 26 May 1973. Of course, Bedford coaches already featured in the fleet.

Bristol MW6G 1832 was given a special livery for a contract service linking Southampton Central station with the BR Seaspeed hoverport, which was alongside the floating bridge chain ferry on the River Itchen. From here a hovercraft service ran to Cowes, Isle of Wight, competing with the Red Funnel hydrofoil service. 1832 was waiting at the station on 6 September 1973.

Not to be outdone, in 1974 rivals Red Funnel had Bristol MW 1833 painted for service 52 from the station to Royal Pier, from whence their ferries departed. 1833 was seen at the garage between duties on 22 April 1975, in company with an MW bus.

Over at Salisbury, former W&D Bristol RELL6G 610 prepares to turn into the bus station. Although it carries a Bournemouth registration mark, as had been the case for vehicles bought since 1969 when the company came under H&D management, its former fleet identity can be determined by the number being in the series below 1000.

Unusual acquisitions in 1973–4 were 3091–4, 160/2–4 AUF, Leyland Leopards with Weymann Castilian C49F bodies, ex-Southdown 1160/2–4. 3093 was at the Battersea coach park in London on 14 September 1974. These carried dual-purpose National livery rather than white coach livery.

In January 1974, the Swanage depot of Western National was transferred to Hants & Dorset along with five Bristol LS buses and one RELL. The RELL, numbered 1652 by H&D, was seen at Poole bus station on 19 August 1978. This was the only single-door, bus-seated RE in the fleet. It will be journeying to Swanage the 'long way' via Wareham rather than by the Sandbanks Ferry.

In 1974–5 the NBC bought lightweight Bedford or Ford chassis for many of its fleets as a quicker delivery alternative to the Bristol LH. Hants & Dorset was one of those who received Ford R1014 buses, which were bodied by ECW. As such, they resembled the LHs but with an RE-style grille, as can be seen on 3582 at Bournemouth in April 1975. The batch 3580–99 and 3801–5 went mostly to Salisbury and Pewsey depots.

In 1974 H&D received some Lodekkas from Southdown, including six of the FSF (short, front entrance) variant new to Brighton, Hove & District. As a result H&D came to operate all four variants of the F series Lodekkas. (FS, FSF, FL, FLF). 3479 was working from Southampton when seen in April 1975.

Also from Southdown came four FS models. This rear view shows the split-level platform that was specified by Brighton, Hove & District to ease boarding.

The early 1970s were a difficult time for bus operators as industrial relations problems in the motor industry led to delays in obtaining spares and new vehicles. Companies had to hire in buses from wherever they could and Hants & Dorset was no exception. Southern Vectis lent ten elderly LD Lodekkas such as LDL 721, seen at Southampton in March 1974 carrying temporary number 3495. The island operator had less need of its fleet in the off-season when there were fewer tourists.

An unusual situation in 1974 was the transfer of Provincial AEC Regent V No. 60 to Hants & Dorset, where it ran as No. 3475. It was used on route 47 Southampton–Winchester via Chandlers Ford, and was caught here between duties at Southampton garage. I have also seen photographic evidence that one of the ex-King Alfred AEC Renowns worked this route as well, although I never saw this myself. Continuing vehicle shortages (not helped by two fires at Basingstoke garage) led to hires from Bournemouth, Southampton and Portsmouth Corporations and Devon General as well.

When the Leyland National was first introduced, only bus-seated versions were produced. But by 1974 dual-purpose examples with coach seating were available and H&D took some of these. 3639 was one of the first of these, seen in Gosport on 13 June 1976 – an appropriate vehicle for the limited-stop service X70 to Southampton.

Five more Leyland Leopards came from North Western in 1975, but these had Alexander Y-type bodies. The first of these, 3095, was photographed at London Zoo on an excursion working in April 1976. It is in dual-purpose livery.

Most coaches were now in National white livery, such as this pair photographed in the parking area at the back of the lower part of the Bournemouth combined bus and coach station. 1057 (REL 741H) is a Bristol RELH6G with Duple body, while 1027 (JEL 426E) is on the shorter RESH6G chassis, again with Duple body. 19 April 1975.

A further five Ford R1014 buses arrived in 1976, but these differed in having Plaxton B43F bodywork. 3812 was at Salisbury, where they were based, in company with an earlier Bristol LH on 2 September 1976.

Tragedy occurred on 25 July 1976 when the combined bus and coach station at Bournemouth was engulfed by fire. Eight Western National coaches and ten H&D vehicles, of which eight were coaches, were destroyed in the conflagration. The damage was considered to be beyond economic repair and the site was later razed to the ground in 1980. Former King Alfred Bedford VAL 2051 is seen at the front of the bus station parking area, with most of the rest fenced off, on 2 September.

With the loss of much of the bus station, Hants & Dorset buses made use of the Triangle, where in earlier days Bournemouth trolleybuses had been parked up. Former Brighton, Hove & District (via Southdown) convertible open-top Bristol FS 3482 is seen here on a service to Sandbanks. Four of these were acquired in 1976 to bring back seasonal open-top operation to this route, which had not seen such vehicles since 1969. Mind you, this one still has its roof on despite it being late July 1977! They retained NBC green livery.

Through the rest of the 1970s Hants & Dorset continued to receive batches of Bristol VRs and Leyland Nationals, standard fare for NBC fleets. 3396, a 1978 VRTSL3/6LXB, leaves Winchester bus station on an ex-King Alfred local service in June 1979. By now the King Alfred AECs and Leyland Tiger Cubs had left the fleet.

Still in use, though, were the three ex-King Alfred Leyland Panthers with Plaxton bodywork and the first of these is entering the bus station on the same day. They would be withdrawn in January 1980 and all saw further service with bus companies in South Wales.

Also still in the fleet were the six Daimler Fleetlines of 1971, despite being the only vehicles of this make. They worked at Poole, where 1906 was found in the bus station on 19 August 1978.

Another five dual-purpose Leyland Nationals came in 1978, Nos 3728–32. 3731 is seen in Southampton when new in 1978.

Despite the influx of new buses, many Lodekkas remained in service, as can be seen here at Southampton's Grosvenor Square garage in August 1978. The two FSs on the right have the Cave-Brown-Cave heating and ventilation equipment with the grilles either side of the destination box. Note also the sun visors over the cab window – a standard specification by H&D for many years. The last Lodekkas, and with them the last conductors, went at Bournemouth in November 1980. At the same time the remaining part of the old fire-damaged bus station closed permanently.

A most unusual vehicle entered service in 1982, towards the end of Hants & Dorset's separate existence. Using the chassis of Bristol LH 3516 (NLJ 516M), a replica charabanc body was constructed by the engineering works at Barton Park, Eastleigh. The resulting vehicle was numbered 86 and registered TR 6147, features previously carried by a 1929 Leyland. This made several rally appearances, including at London Transport's Chiswick Works on 2 July 1983.

The Shamrock & Rambler coach fleet had been hived off to National Travel South West in 1973, but in 1981 it was handed back, although of course the vehicles had changed. One of the vehicles received was 3017 (PDG 112M), a 1974 Leyland Leopard PSU3B/4RT with Plaxton body. This is seen on the road network surrounding Gatwick Airport, about to take up a journey to Bournemouth on 7 March 1982. This attractive blue, orange and white livery was adopted.

Following the NBC's Market Analysis Project (MAP) surveys from 1978 onwards, local marketing names were adopted. The Fareham area routes, both H&D and Provincial, gained the 'Provincial' brand from 1980. Hence we see H&D Bristol RELL6G No. 1651 with Provincial lettering. This was taken in London, near Victoria, on 10 July 1982. There was a national rail strike, and any available vehicles were being drafted in as relief vehicles for National Express services.

Hampshire Bus 1983–5

Hants & Dorset acquired a batch of twenty ex-London Daimler Fleetlines with MCW bodies in 1983 and these passed to both Hampshire Bus and Wilts & Dorset. Hampshire Bus OJD 194R, ex-London Transport DMS2194, stands at Southampton Central station on 5 July 1983. They were all converted to single-door before entering service.

Basingstoke, once the province of the old Wilts & Dorset, now came in Hampshire Bus territory. Bristol VR 3438 departs on a local service on 5 July 1983.

At the same location, Leyland National 3735 carries an overall advert for Freedom Tickets.

Three Plaxton-bodied Bristol RELH coaches were acquired from City of Oxford in 1983 to inaugurate the 727 service between Southampton and Portsmouth using the new M27 motorway. The service was worked jointly with Southdown. No. 174, seen departing from Southampton bus station on 5 July, however, still shows blinds from its previous owner.

Coach-seated VR 3343 departs Winchester for Southampton on 15 September 1984.

A Bristol LH backs out of the stand at Southampton bus station with a service to Romsey on 16 June 1984. Originally Bristol No. 439, this was part of a batch transferred to Hants & Dorset in 1981. These replaced older vehicles and the non-standard Fords.

Coaches were run under the Hampshire Coach name. 3063 (SRU 148R), a 1977 Leyland Leopard with Plaxton body, had passed to Shamrock & Rambler in 1983 but came back in 1984. Here it departs Heathrow Airport for Salisbury on National Express duties, 14 June 1984.

At the bus rally held in the grounds of the former Netley Military Hospital on 7 July 1985, new Leyland Tiger coach 180 was on display. It carried a Plaxton forty-eight-seat body.

Wilts & Dorset 1983–5

Bournemouth and Poole, both now in Dorset, became part of the territory of the revived Wilts & Dorset company. Bristol VR 3416, photographed in Bournemouth in July 1985, was one of six that came from Southern Vectis on the Isle of Wight in 1979 in exchange for convertible open-top VRs that had been bought but not used as such by H&D.

Ex-London Daimler Fleetlines entered the new Wilts & Dorset fleet and former DM1239 (KUC 239P) was based at Poole garage, where it was seen on 6 July 1985.

The six original Fleetlines of 1971 were also at Poole, where 1904 was noted on the same occasion.

Former Bristol Omnibus LH 3825 carried route branding for the Poole Quay Shuttle service. Another LH, just visible behind, carried a special livery for the route.

The new Wilts & Dorset did not treat its single-deckers to the dignity of a white band to relieve the monotony of poppy red. Bristol RELL 1635 is at its home garage of Poole, denoted by the white spot garage code. The evening light makes the livery appear orange.

The cutaway front of this Bristol LH, seen at Swanage station, shows that it is one of those specially adapted for crossing on the Sandbanks Ferry. A batch of 'M'-registered LHs had replaced the Bedford VAMs on this service in 1974, and they were replaced by these 1980-built buses in 1981.

Overall advertising was increasingly popular in the 1970s and 1980s. Bristol VR 3338 promotes a local model village and amusement park.

Another VR in advertising livery, No. 3405 loads at Weymouth for the service back to Bournemouth on 6 July 1985.

Resplendently painted in the old pre-NBC Wilts & Dorset livery, Bristol RELL 1615 (actually a former Hants & Dorset bus) was an exhibit at the Showbus rally held at Woburn on 1 September 1985.

The first vehicles bought new by the Wilts & District company were five Leyland Olympian ONLXB/1R with ECW coach-seated bodies in 1984. The coach seats of 3903 will be appreciated by the passengers as the bus was pressed onto a National Express service for Bristol when seen leaving Victoria Coach Station on 20 April 1984.

Also new in 1984 were ten Leyland Tigers with Duple coach bodywork. 3209 was at Battersea in July 1985.

Shamrock & Rambler/Pilgrim Coaches 1983–5

A pair of Shamrock & Rambler coaches at Southampton Central station on 5 July 1983. 3054, a Plaxton-bodied Leyland Leopard, sports the livery applied under H&D ownership. The vehicle behind carries the colours in an NBC style.

The NBC-style livery is seen to better effect on 3039, a Duple-bodied Leopard that was originally new to National Travel South West. It is leaving Heathrow bus station on a service from London to Bournemouth with what appears to be a full load on 14 June 1984.

The replica charabanc passed to Shamrock & Rambler and was repainted orange. In its new guise it visited the Sandwell rally at West Bromwich on 13 May 1984.

Shamrock & Rambler 3125 was one of a pair of Bova Futura coaches bought in 1984 to provide transport for the Bournemouth orchestras (Bournemouth Symphony Orchestra and Sinfonietta). They were given non-year-specific registrations 125 EJU and 124 YTW. However, on this occasion it has been drafted in on National Express service and is laying over at Battersea on 25 August 1984 before returning from London to Bournemouth.

From 23 January 1984 the Southampton-based part of the fleet was hived off as Pilgrim Coaches. Seen arriving at Victoria Coach Station on 29 April 1984, No. 77 was a Duple-bodied Leyland Leopard, ex-S&R and H&D 3091 but originally new to Grant, Fareham.

Seen in Southampton in July 1985, Pilgrim Coaches 85, AAD 185S, was a Duple-bodied Leyland Leopard that had already been lettered for National Travel South West and Shamrock & Rambler. Now it was carrying branding on behalf of Townsend Thoresen, who ran a car ferry service to France from Southampton Docks.

Provincial (Gosport & Fareham)

Provincial was noted for its Guy Arab buses fitted with Deutz air-cooled engines and bodywork by Readings of Portsmouth. HHA 84 was a 1945 Arab II which started life as Midland Red No. 2589. The body dated from 1964. This was photographed at Gosport Ferry on 17 October 1970.

The last of the Guy Arab/Deutz buses and the only single-decker was No. 37. This had a 1967 registration, but its origins were much older. The body may have dated from then, but the chassis was a Guy Arab III originally with United Welsh and registered HCY 296. It was constructed for the Fareham–Knowle route but was photographed at Gosport Ferry on 21 January 1972. It would be withdrawn later that year along with the double-deck versions.

More conventional Guys were seven 1948 Arab IIIs with Park Royal bodywork from the extensive fleet once owned by Southampton. FCR 445 approaches the Gosport terminus on 17 October 1970.

FCR 445 again, at the Gosport terminus adjacent to the pier for the ferry service across to Portsmouth on 8 May 1971. This was previously Southampton No. 144.

In 1968 Provincial bought nine Seddon Pennine IV buses with Strachans B40D bodies. No. 39 represents the type.

These were followed in 1969 by six more, but these had Pennine bodies (a subsidiary of Seddon).

One of the first actions under NBC ownership was the drafting in of some Bristol LS buses from other NBC fleets (plus one Bristol SUL). Two dual-purpose LS6Gs came from Midland General in 1970. Former Midland General 241 became Provincial 35.

The double-deck fleet was refreshed with seven AEC Regent Vs from Oxford. 977 CWL, with Park Royal bodywork, was formerly Oxford 977.

The first new vehicles for the fleet under NBC ownership came in 1971 when six Bristol RELL6Gs entered the fleet. Originally, Daimler Fleetlines had been ordered but these were diverted to Hants & Dorset in exchange for the RELLs (see p. 20). BCG 103J is seen at Gosport and displays the later style livery and fleetname. A further six RELLS followed in 1972, diverted from Northern General.

Three 1965 Duple-bodied Bedford SB13 coaches were transferred from Wilts & Dorset in 1971–2. BMW 135C is seen on a National Express relief service at the back of Victoria Coach Station on 10 August 1974.

On 9 November 1972 a new bus station opened at Gosport Ferry, replacing the somewhat primitive facilities provided beforehand. The first Leyland Nationals were delivered in time to promote this, and these would be followed by further batches thereafter until 1983. 16 (HOR 416L) was one of the first batch of five seen at the new bus station on 22 March 1973. All of the Provincial Leyland Nationals had dual doors, as did the RELLs.

Two Marshall-bodied Leyland Leopards came from Southdown in 1972. No. 29 was at Gosport on the same day.

Now in NBC green, Bristol RELL No. 2 is seen at the new bus station on 5 September 1973.

The Seddons were still in use, painted into NBC green. Strachan-bodied No. 39 pulls away from the stands at Gosport.

Although no longer in passenger service, the Guys had not fully departed. Former Red & White HWO 344, a Duple-bodied veteran from 1949, survived as a trainer. One of two acquired, its fellow, HWO 334, would later pass into preservation at the Wythall Bus Museum.

A visit to Hoeford garage on 15 June 1976 found Seddon 44 going nowhere quickly – it had been stripped of parts to keep others on the road.

Others were still active though, including No. 42.

Also at the garage was former King Alfred Bedford VAL EOU 703D, transferred along with VAM JHO 702E to the Provincial fleet in 1976.

A number of Bristol LH buses were transferred from Hants & Dorset between 1977 and 1981. REL 744H came in 1977 and was lettered for an Asda free service. It was at Hoeford garage on 11 June 1978.

Another of the LHs, also at Hoeford garage.

Leyland National 23 and a former Brighton, Hove & District Lodekka, which had replaced the Guy Arab trainer by this time.

To celebrate the centenary of the original Gosport & Fareham company, Bristol RELL6G No. 10 was renumbered 100 and painted in original Provincial livery. It featured at the Southsea Rally held on 11 June 1978.

By the 1980s, Leyland Nationals dominated the fleet. This 1976 example was laying over in Gosport bus station on 14 June 1981.

Two of the National 2 models entered the fleet in 1980. No. 45 approaches journey's end at Gosport on 14 June 1981.

Provincial 1983–5

When Hants & Dorset was split up in April 1983, the Fareham area services and vehicles of H&D passed to Provincial. These were already marketed under the Provincial name as a result of the MAP project. The revised Provincial bus company was a larger and far different outfit to that inherited by the NBC in 1969. The 1983 fleet consisted entirely of single-deck vehicles – Bristol RELLs, LHs and Leyland Nationals. The oldest bus dated from 1969, and most dated from 1972 onwards.

We saw Bristol RELL XLJ 726K before, under Hants & Dorset ownership, but with Provincial fleetname (see p. 49). Here it is again, now owned by Provincial and repainted in National green and white. It is departing Southampton for Fareham on what would have been an H&D service in the past. Quite a healthy load on board too! 5 July 1983.

At Winchester, Leyland National 70 is backed out at the commencement of a journey to Fareham on ex-H&D route 69. This was one of seventeen Leyland Nationals, Nos 60–76, that transferred from Hants & Dorset. 16 June 1984.

Southdown

Unlike Hants & Dorset, Southdown was an early convert to the Bristol VR, taking the early flat-fronted version. 2097, delivered in 1969, was from a batch that had been ordered by Brighton, Hove & District. It was seen in Portsmouth on 20 November 1972.

From 7 March 1976 the new 'Solenteer' service X71, worked jointly with Hants & Dorset, connected Southampton with Portsmouth and Southsea. Southdown used Leyland Atlanteans with route branding, while H&D used similarly branded VRs. 745 (LCD 45P) was on the route at Southampton bus station on 3 July 1977.

Another of the Southdown 'Solenteer' Atlanteans at Southsea, although on this occasion it is working on a different service. 11 June 1978.

Southdown Bristol VR 685 at Southsea on the limited-stop service for Southampton, now modified and renumbered X16. Note the 'limited stop' slipboard on the front. 14 June 1981.

Southdown reached west as far as Fareham. One of the famous 'Queen Mary' Leyland PD3s was noted at Provincial's Hoeford garage for school bus duties on 11 June 1978.

Western National 1970–82

Western National Bristol LS5G No. 1769 stands at Swanage station on 22 January 1972. In January 1974 five of these buses (though not this one) and one RELL would pass to Hants & Dorset when the Swanage outstation was transferred to the Hampshire-based company.

Western National reached both Bournemouth and Salisbury on joint routes. Seen at Salisbury bus station on the long through route from Weymouth is 3011, a 1959 dual-purpose Bristol MW6G that had come from Mansfield District in 1974.

Western National Bristol LH No. 760 on the seafront at Weymouth, working a local town service on 18 June 1973.

A pair of Bristol FLF Lodekkas at Weymouth on 3 July 1977 contrast the earlier and later radiator designs.

1970-built Bristol LH 758 stands alongside a Leyland National on the same day.

A pair of later LHs with the curved front windscreen later adopted by ECW.

AEC Reliance 42 with Marshall bodywork was formerly with BET company Devon General. Devon General had been placed under Western National control from 1 January 1971, although retaining its own name and (later) NBC poppy red livery. However, inter-fleet transfers would occur, as in this case. 2 July 1978.

Inside Weymouth garage was one of the ex-Devon General 'Sea Dog' convertible open-top Leyland Atlanteans, No. 927 *Sir Martin Frobisher*. It had been transferred to work the coastal service to Bridport along what is now marketed as the Jurassic Coast. 2 July 1978.

Still active in July 1979 is Reliance No. 42, seen alongside VR 1111.

Another VR is active on the seafront with a local service. Note the advert for Wanderbus tickets, a bargain at £2.40.

Western National FLF No. 2080 was painted in Sealink colours and was displayed at the bus rally being held in the town on 1 July 1979 (and the reason I was visiting).

Also taking part in the rally was the former Southern National's first Bristol LS 1701 of 1953, now preserved. This vehicle now forms part of the Science Museum collection, housed at Wroughton airfield near Swindon.

Western National celebrated fifty years in 1979 by painting VR 1097 in this special livery. It was displayed at the rally held in Weymouth on 1 July.

Southern National 1983–5

A standard Southern National VR No. 1161 in Weymouth on 6 July 1985.

The fleet also contained convertible open-top VRs. These had been purchased to replace the Devon General Atlanteans. No. 942 *Lawrence of Arabia* seeks custom on a hot, sunny 6 July on Weymouth seafront. The green and cream livery is a distinct improvement on National green.

These Marshall-bodied Bristol LHs had been a unique purchase by Royal Blue. Following a time-honoured tradition, 1316 has been downgraded for bus work and is painted in bus livery, although retaining coach seats.

Border Visitors – Aldershot & District/Alder Valley

Aldershot & District worked route 14 into Winchester from Aldershot via Alton, paralleling the Mid-Hants railway, closed by BR in 1973. Marshall-bodied AEC Reliance 571 was seen on 24 August 1969. This was a Sunday – Dennis Lolines worked the route between Monday and Saturday.

Aldershot & District were merged with Thames Valley to form Alder Valley from 1 January 1972. Dennis Loline III AAA 521C is in the short-lived maroon livery that was adopted before NBC poppy red took over. 7 March 1973.

By contrast, 465 EOT carries the NBC red livery that would replace the old colours. It also has Alexander rather than Weymann bodywork. Aldershot & District specified sliding rather than folding doors on its Dennis Loline IIIs.

By September 1976 Leyland Nationals could be found and the 214, as the route had now become, extended to Guildford.

The same location seen in June 1979 but this time the service is being worked by a coach-seated Bristol VR, No. 930 (HPK 507N).

Conventional Bristol VR 940 is rostered on this occasion in September 1984.

Aldershot & District/Alder Valley also worked into Basingstoke. Alder Valley RESL6G 448 is still in Aldershot & District identity on 24 March 1972. Although A&D was a BET company, the Bristol/ECW combination had been available on the open market since 1968 and several BET fleets had specified these, including the Guildford-based company, who had previously favoured AECs.

Border Visitors – Bristol

Bristol had joint routes with Wilts & Dorset into Salisbury from Trowbridge and Swindon. Dual-purpose Bristol RELH6L No. 2047 had arrived from Trowbridge on 16 May 1971. The Trowbridge area routes were transferred from Western National to Bristol in 1971, so prior to this the route had been joint with WNOC.

Visiting Coaches – Royal Blue and Other NBC Companies

Express services to Southampton and all points west were provided by Royal Blue, the coaching arm of Western National. The coach station at Winchester, alongside the cattle market, was a refreshment stop for these and hosts of other coaches, especially before the motorways and their service areas took over.

Royal Blue Bristol RELH6G No. 1457 stands at Victoria Coach Station with a relief service for Southampton before the roof was extended over this part of the coach station. 10 April 1971.

A pair of Royal Blue Bristol RELH coaches take a break at Winchester coach station on 8 September 1973. No. 2353 on the right is in the later reversed livery of white with a blue stripe, while 2388 is in the National white which would replace the individual coach liveries of the 1960s.

Royal Blue 1310 was a 1970 Bristol LH6L with Duple C41F body. It was also seen at Winchester coach station, in this case on 4 August 1973.

Greenslades of Exeter 403, a Harrington Cavalier-bodied AEC Reliance was working on hire to Royal Blue and painted in its livery. This was at the coach station on 8 September 1973. Greenslades would become one of the constituents of National Travel South West from 1 April 1974.

A newer Royal Blue coach, 2421, a 1974 Bristol RELH6Lwith Plaxton body, shows blinds for tour duties at Weymouth garage on 1 July 1979. This would later pass to Southern National when the Western National fleet was split up in 1983.

With the split of Western National, Southern National took on the National Express service from London to Weymouth. No. 131, a 1977 Leyland Leopard PSU3E/4R with Willowbrook body, lays over at Battersea on 25 May 1983. Acquired with the split from Western National, it had started out with National Travel South West.

Before the motorway network was fully established, a major coach interchange point was at the St Margaret's Cheltenham coach station of Black & White Motorways. Coaches would congregate here from all over the country to interchange before making mass departures. The 2.00 p.m. departure was the main event of the day. However, the motorways made this connecting point obsolete and the coach station was run-down and used as a bus garage in the 1970s, finally closing and becoming a car park in 1985. Black & White Motorways 141, a Leyland Leopard with Duple Northern body, originally with Western Welsh, is at the Southampton coach station on 13 February 1973.

When Shamrock & Rambler was taken over by the THC in 1966, only the Southampton-based fleet passed to Hants & Dorset in 1969. The Bournemouth-based fleet remained separate until becoming a constituent of National Travel South West in April 1974. Duple-bodied Bedford VAL PEL 997G *Swift* was photographed in Exeter bus and coach station on 4 June 1971.

MHL 226F *Whyle* was a 1968 Bedford VAM70 with Plaxton bodywork, ex-Hebble 34. It was spotted in Winchester on 1 August 1973, looking quite anonymous in National white.

Another Bedford VAL, also by now in National white, was VLJ 233J *Raven*, seen here at the Southampton H&D garage on 3 July 1977. It was now part of National Travel South West, though still retaining S&R fleetname.

Hebble was a name that would disappear as it was absorbed into National Travel North East in 1974. No. 47 (EHD 522F), an Alexander-bodied Leyland Leopard new to Yorkshire Woollen District, was working back to Bradford when it called into Winchester on 16 September 1973.

On the same day was East Midland C61, a 1963 Leyland Leopard PSU3/3RT with Plaxton bodywork.

Southdown had an extensive coach fleet. LCD 238F, a Plaxton-bodied Leyland Leopard, pauses for a break before returning home to Eastbourne.

Seen in Portsmouth are three of Southdown's many Leyland Tiger Cub coaches. This batch, 1130–1154, with Weymann bodywork dated from 1959–61. Taken on 22 March 1973.

South Midland had been a coaching arm of THC fleet Thames Valley, serving Oxford–London, until the NBC transferred it to former BET fleet City of Oxford in 1971. Bristol RELH6G 22 shows the Oxford/South Midland fleetname then adopted. Seen at Winchester on 8 September 1973.

Seen in Winchester bus station rather than the coach station, XEH 129M was a 1973 Ford R1114 with Duple fifty-three-seat body, an uncommon choice for an NBC company. 29 September 1973.

At Southampton on an excursion in June 1972, Maidstone & District 4021 was a 1962 AEC Reliance fitted with just thirty-seven seats for touring.

Acknowledgements and Bibliography

Aish, Norman, *Buses in Camera: South West* (Shepperton; Ian Allan, 1977).

Fereday Glenn, D., *Bus Operators 3: Hants & Dorset* (Shepperton: Ian Allen, 1985).

Hypher, John, *Glory Days: Wilts & Dorset* (Hersham: Ian Allen, 2007).

Keeley, Malcolm and Paul Gray, *British Bus Celebration: South Central England* (Harrow Weald: Capital Transport, 1984).

Prince, James, *Glory Days: Hants & Dorset* (Hersham: Ian Allen, 2006).

Buses (Shepperton/Hersham: Ian Allen) monthly magazine.

Various fleetlists published by The PSV Circle.